Ukulele 1 Songbook

INTRODUCTION

Welcome back to FastTrack®!

Hope you enjoyed *Ukulele 1* and are ready to play some hits. Have you and your friends formed a band? Or do you feel like soloing with the audio tracks? Either way, get ready...it's time to jam!

The eight songs in this book use notes and chords you learned in *Ukulele 1*, so you're already ahead of the game! Feel free to play either the melody notes or strum the chords, but don't forget the three **P**s: **P**atience, **P**ractice and **P**ace yourself.

As with *Ukulele 1*, don't try to bite off more than you can chew. If you get frustrated, put down your uke, relax and just listen to the audio. If you forget a chord or note position, go back and learn it. If you're doing fine, think about booking a gig!

ABOUT THE AUDIO

Each track is preceded by count-off "clicks" to help you feel the beat before the music starts. If the tempo (speed) is too fast for you, no problem! You can slow it down without changing the pitch. If you want to focus on a tricky part, you can set loop points to play it over and over. Pan right to hear the ukulele part emphasized. Pan left to hear the accompaniment emphasized.

PLAYBACK+
Speed • Pitch • Balance • Loop

To access audio visit:
www.halleonard.com/mylibrary

Enter Code
6358-5497-3374-5131

ISBN 978-1-4950-6153-0

HAL•LEONARD®
CORPORATION

7777 W. BLUEMOUND RD. P.O. BOX 13819 MILWAUKEE, WI 53213

Visit Hal Leonard Online at
www.halleonard.com

LEARN SOMETHING NEW EACH DAY

We know you're eager to play, but first we need to explain a few things. We'll make it brief—just one page...

Song Structure

Most songs have different sections, which might be indicated by any or all of the following labels:

 INTRODUCTION (or "intro"): This is a short section at the beginning that (you guessed it!) introduces the song to the listeners.

 VERSES: One of the main sections of a song is the **verse**. There will often be several verses, all with the same music, but each with different lyrics.

 CHORUS: Another main section of a song is the **chorus**. There might be several choruses, but each one will usually have the same lyrics and music.

 BRIDGE: This section makes a transition from one part of a song to the next. For example, you may find a bridge between the chorus and the next verse.

 OUTRO: Similar to the "intro," this section brings the song to an end.

Endings

1st and 2nd Endings

These are indicated by brackets and numbers:

Simply play the song through to the first ending, then repeat back to the first repeat sign or the beginning of the song (whichever is the case). Play through the song again, but skip the first ending and play the second ending.

D.S. al Coda

When you see these words, go back and repeat from this symbol: 𝄋

Play until you see the words "*To Coda*" and skip to the Coda, indicated by this symbol: 𝄌

Now just finish the song.

D.S. al Fine

Just like D.S. al Coda, go back to the 𝄋 symbol. Play until you see the word **Fine** (pronounced "FEE-nay"). It's an Italian word that means "the end," so now you've finished the song.

OK, you're good to go! Enjoy the music...

CONTENTS

A Teenager in Love

Words by Doc Pomus
Music by Mort Shuman

Bridge

I cried a tear for no - bod - y but you.

D.C. al Coda

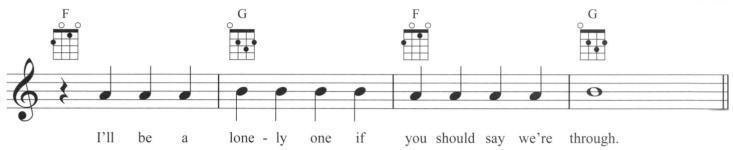

I'll be a lone - ly one if you should say we're through.

Coda

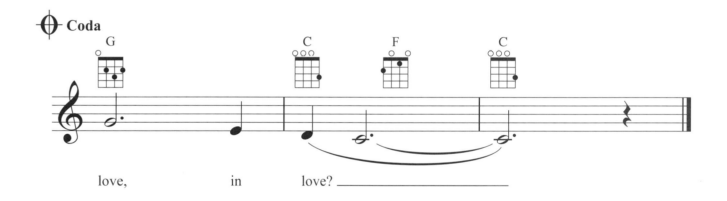

love, in love? _____

Additional Lyrics

2. One day I feel so happy, next day I feel so sad.
   I guess I'll learn to take the good with the bad.

3. If you want to make me cry, that won't be so hard to do.
   And if you should say goodbye, I'll still go on loving you.

Bad Moon Rising

Words and Music by John Fogerty

First note

Verse
Moderately fast

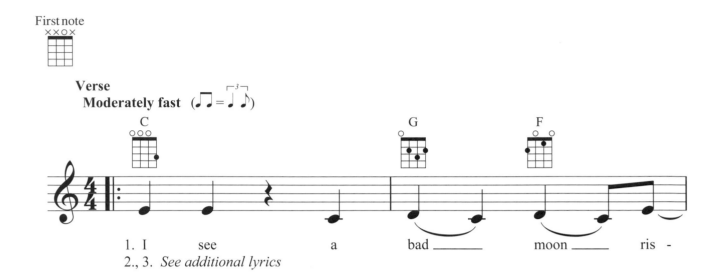

1. I see a bad _____ moon _____ ris -
2., 3. *See additional lyrics*

- in'. I see

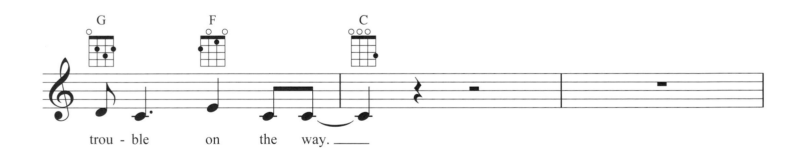

trou - ble on the way. _____

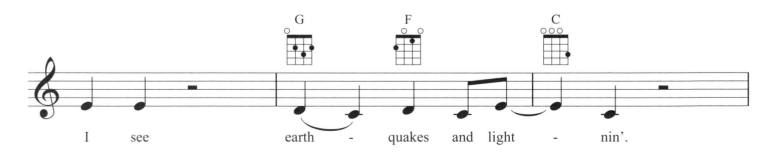

I see earth - quakes and light - nin'.

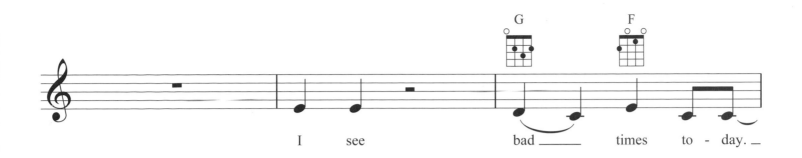

I see   bad _____ times   to - day. _

%: **Chorus**

_____   Don't   go   a - round   to - night. _

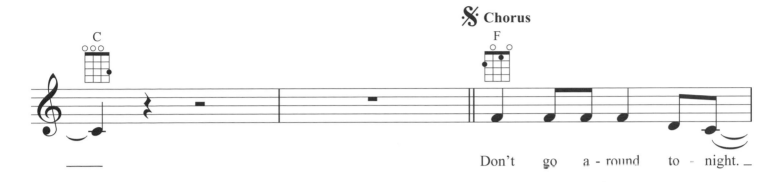

_____   Well, it's   bound   to   take _ your   life. _____

To Coda

There's   a   bad _____ moon   on   the   rise. _____

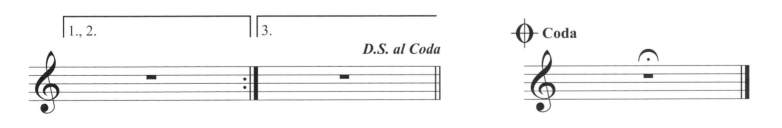

|1., 2. |3.

D.S. al Coda

Coda

Additional Lyrics

2. I hear hurricanes a-blowin'.
   I know the end is comin' soon.
   I fear rivers overflowin'.
   I hear the voice of rage and ruin.

3. Hope you got your things together.
   Hope you are quite prepared to die.
   Looks like we're in for nasty weather.
   One eye is taken for an eye.

Chasing Cars

Words and Music by Gary Lightbody, Tom Simpson, Paul Wilson, Jonathan Quinn and Nathan Connolly

or an - y - one. ___

then not ___ e - nough. ___

to find ___ my ___ own. ___

Chorus

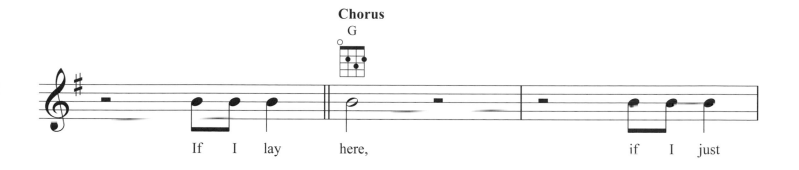

If I lay here, if I just

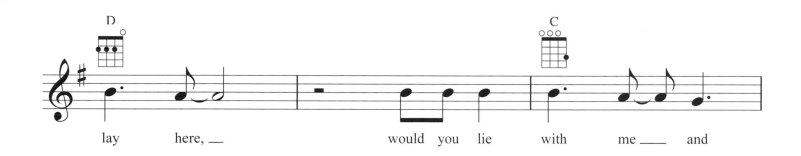

lay here, ___ would you lie with me ___ and

1.

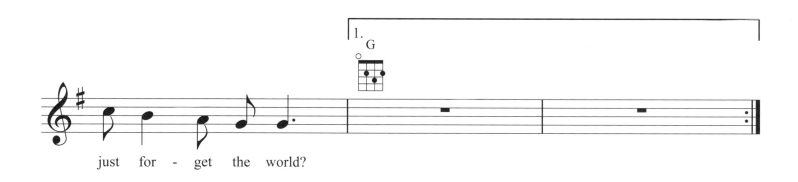

just for - get the world?

2., 3.   **Bridge 1**

For - get what we're told

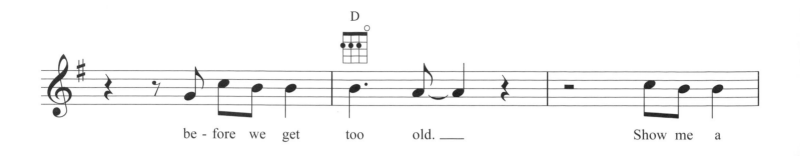

be - fore we get too old. ___ Show me a

gar - den ___ that's burst - ing in - to life.

D.C. al Coda
(take 2nd ending)

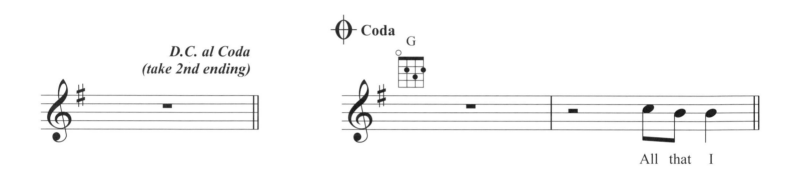

Coda G

All that I

Bridge 2

am, all that I ev - er was ___

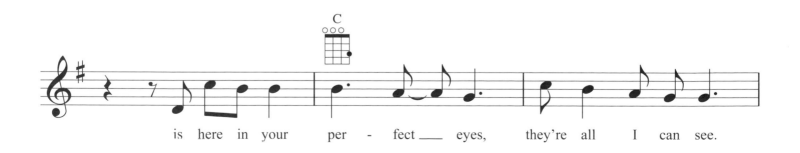

is here in your per - fect ___ eyes, they're all I can see.

I don't know where,

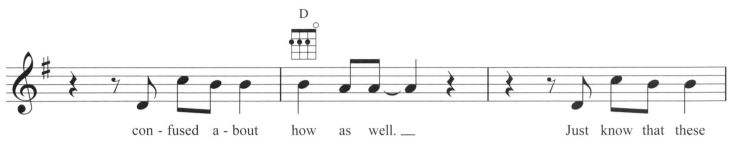

con - fused a - bout how as well. ___ Just know that these

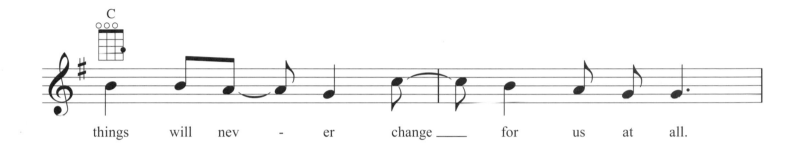

things will nev - er change ___ for us at all.

Outro-Chorus

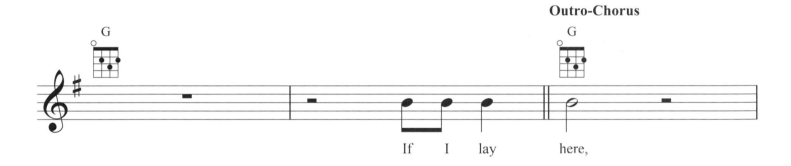

If I lay here,

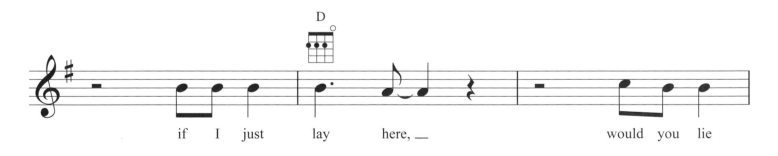

if I just lay here, ___ would you lie

with me ___ and just for - get the world?

Mr. Tambourine Man

Words and Music by Bob Dylan

First note

Chorus
Moderately fast

Hey, Mis - ter Tam - bou - rine ___ Man,

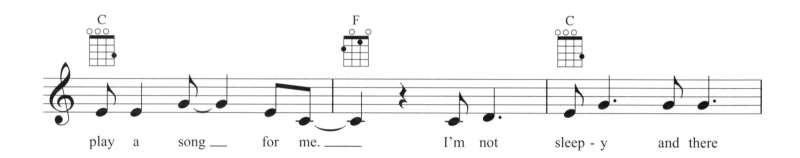

play a song ___ for me. ___ I'm not sleep - y and there

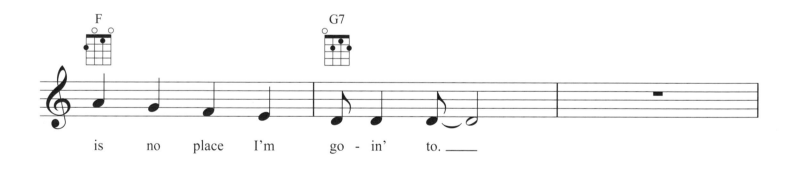

is no place I'm go - in' to. ___

Hey, Mis - ter Tam - bou - rine ___ Man, play a song ___ for me. ___

In the jin - gle jan - gle morn - in', I'll come

fol - low - in' you.

Fine

1. Though I
2.–4. *See additional lyrics*

Verse

know that eve - nin's em - pire _____ has re - turned in - to

sand, van - ished from ___ my hand, left me

blind - ly here to stand, but still not sleep - in'. _____

My wea - ri - ness ___ a - maz - es me, ___ I'm

13

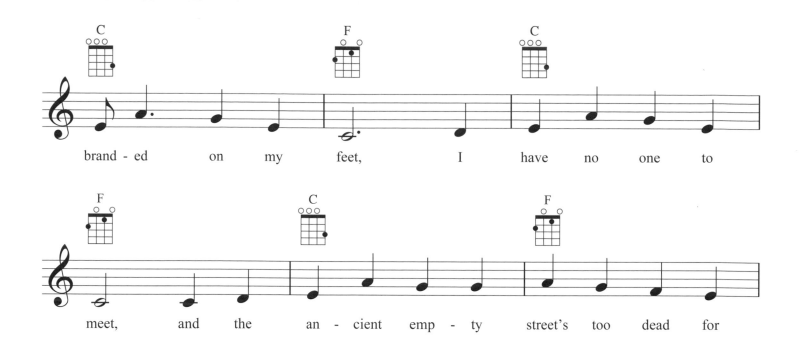

brand - ed   on   my   feet,   I   have   no   one   to

meet,   and   the   an - cient   emp - ty   street's   too   dead   for

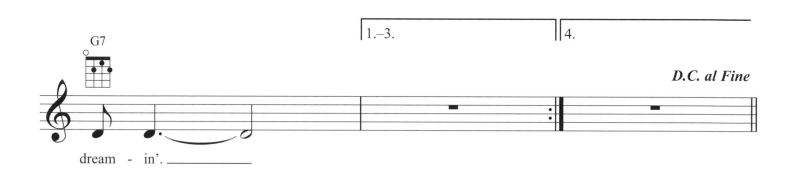

1.–3.   4.

D.C. al Fine

dream - in'. _____

Additional Lyrics

2. Take me on a trip upon your magic swirlin' ship.
   My senses have been stripped, my hands can't feel to grip.
   My toes too numb to step, wait only for my boot heels to be wanderin'.
   I'm ready to go anywhere, I'm ready for to fade
   Into my own parade, cast your dancin' spell my way.
   I promise to go under it.

3. Though you might hear laughin', spinnin', swingin' madly across the sun,
   It's not aimed at anyone, it's just escapin' on the run.
   And but for the sky, there are no fences facin',
   And if you hear vague traces of skippin' reels of rhyme
   To your tambourine in time, it's just a ragged clown behind.
   I wouldn't pay it any mind; it's just a shadow you're seein' that he's chasin'.

4. Then take me disappearin' through the smoke rings of my mind,
   Down the foggy ruins of time, far past the frozen leaves,
   The haunted, frightened trees out to the windy beach,
   Far from the twisted reach of crazy sorrow,
   Yes, to dance beneath the diamond sky with one hand wavin' free,
   Silhouetted by the sea, circled by the circus sands,
   With all memory and fate driven deep beneath the waves.
   Let me forget about today until tomorrow.

This page is intentionally left blank to avoid unnecessary page turns.

My Heart Will Go On

(Love Theme from 'Titanic')

from the Paramount and Twentieth Century Fox Motion Picture TITANIC

Music by James Horner
Lyric by Will Jennings

§ Chorus

(1., 2.) Near,   far,   wher - ev - er you are, ___
(D.S.) You're   here;   there's noth - ing I fear, ___

___ I be - lieve that the heart does go on. ___
___ and I know that my heart will go on. ___

___ Once more you o - pen the door, ___
___ We'll stay for - ev - er this way. ___

___ and you're here in my heart, and my heart will go
___ You are safe in my heart, and my heart will go

To Coda ⊕   *2nd time, D.S. al Coda*

on and on.
on and

⊕ **Coda**

on.   Mm. ___

Good Riddance
(Time of Your Life)

Words by Billie Joe
Music by Green Day

Verse
Moderately fast

1. An - oth - er turn - ing point, __ a fork __ __ stuck in __ the __ road. __ the wrist, __ di - rects __ you where __ to __ go. So make the best ___ of __ this test ___ and don't __ ask why. __

2. So take the pho - to - graphs __ and still - - frames in __ your __ mind. __ a shelf __ in good __ health and __ good __ time. Tat - toos of mem - o - ries and dead __ skin __ on trial. __

Time grabs you by __ Hang it on __

It's not a ques - tion, but __ a les -
For what it's worth, __ it __ was worth

Rocky Top

Words and Music by Boudleaux Bryant and Felice Bryant

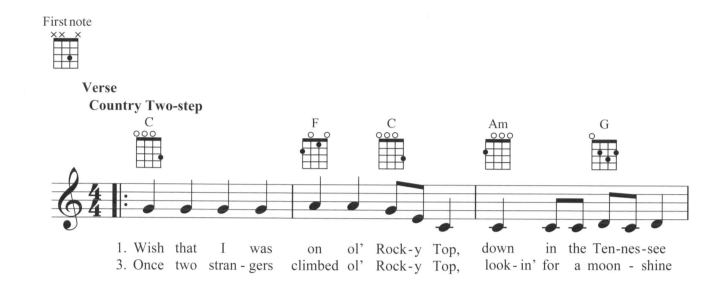

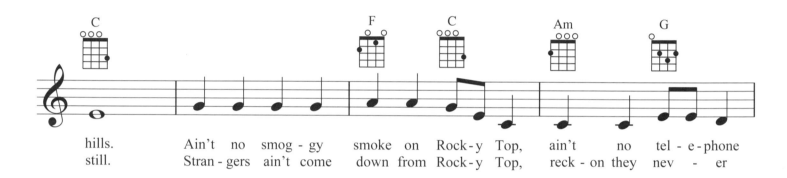

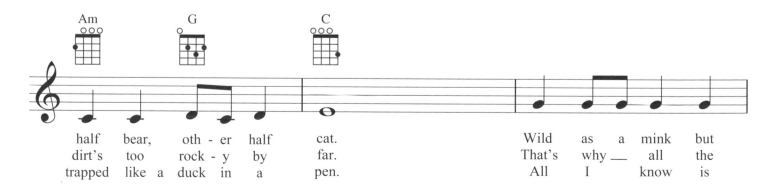

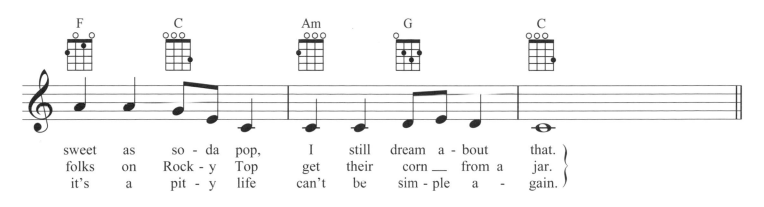

sweet as so-da pop, I still dream a-bout that.
folks on Rock-y Top get their corn — from a jar.
it's a pit-y life can't be sim-ple a - gain.

Chorus

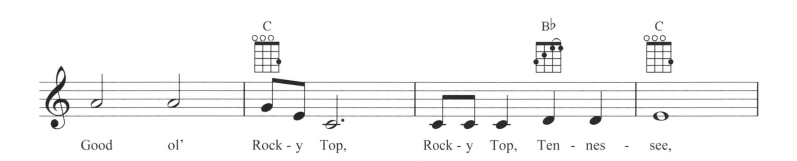

Rock-y Top, you'll al - ways be home sweet home to me.

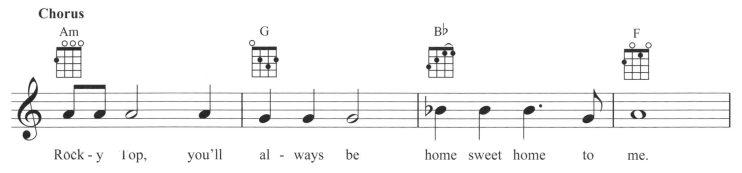

Good ol' Rock-y Top, Rock-y Top, Ten - nes - see,

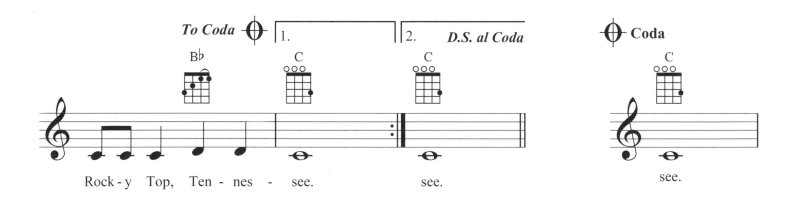

To Coda ⊕ 1. 2. *D.S. al Coda* ⊕ Coda

Rock-y Top, Ten - nes - see. see. see.

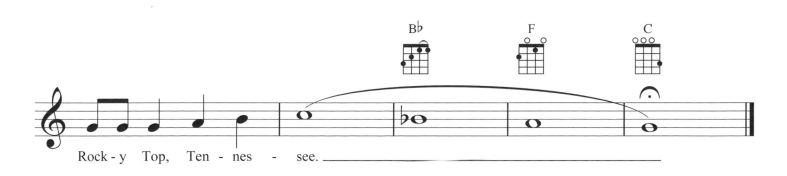

Rock-y Top, Ten - nes - see. _____

Fly Like an Eagle

Words and Music by Steve Miller

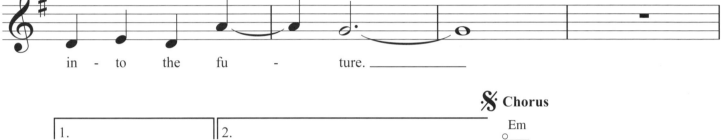

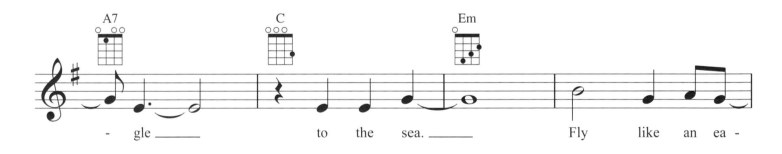

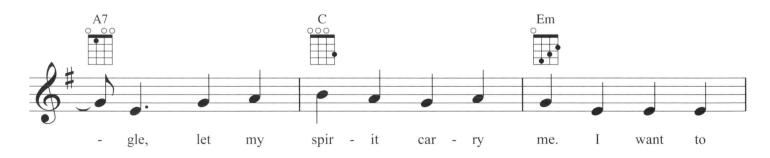

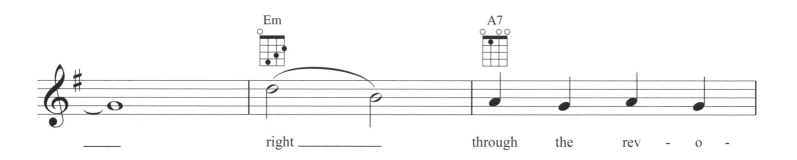

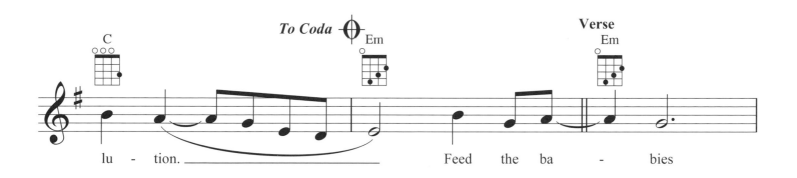

House the peo - ple

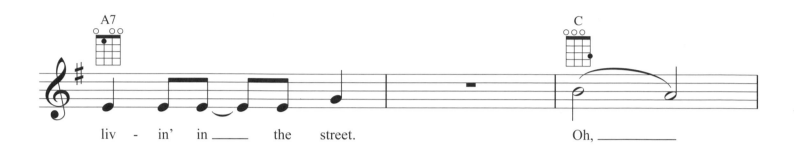

A7

C

liv - in' in _____ the street.

Oh, _____

Em

D.S. al Coda

there's a so - lu - tion.

I wan - na fly _____

Coda

Em

Outro

Em

_____

Time keeps on slip - pin', slip - pin',

slip - pin' _____

in - to the fu - ture. _____

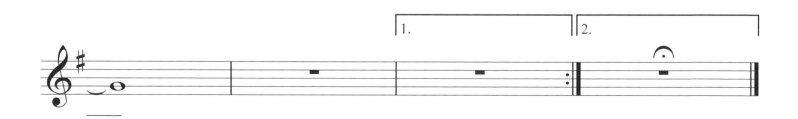

1.

2.

_____